The Butter Knife And The Nutcracker

John Ian

BookLeaf Publishing

Presentation by *BookLeaf Publishing*

Web: www.bookleafpub.com

E-mail: info@bookleafpub.com

ISBN: 9789357212618

First edition 2023

For Sylvia, who motivated me to do this

PREFACE

This collection of poems is the result of a writing challenge: One poem a day for three weeks, to be published as is, right after those 21 days. And the challenge was taken seriously, only a minimal amount of editing was done.

In that sense this little book was also an exercise in letting go and in acceptance. Releasing something out into the world in the raw, with all its imperfections.

Untroubled

Nothing but trouble
Then nothing but
Then but
Then nothing

And the trouble
Question mark

The question marked the end
Then silence

Tug Of War

When summer started on this tender note
It was time to leave
As there was nothing left to run away from

In an instant he knew
He needed to
Let go of the rope

The Butter Knife And The Nutcracker

So smooth, it doesn't hurt one bit
So soft
So effortless

Closed-minded concepts cracked
Open
The core, the root, everything
Suddenly so obvious

This shell
A small crack
Would Christmas be a good time?
Walnuts really do look like tiny brains

Kitchen Table

The conversation at the kitchen table
Came with an unexpected twist
He tried to smile but wasn't able
And left her waiting lips unkissed

He gave a questionable answer
She wore a fashionable dress
Back in the day she could have been a dancer
But they said she was too eager to impress

The coffee cold, time moving slowly
A deeper sense of something more
What comes and goes is never holy
Leaves only silence to explore

Loss

So truthfully he makes the vow and leaves to
sign the deal
So skillfully she breaks the fruit and strips away
the peel
So silently, friend, autumn comes and takes it all
away
He takes it all, she takes it all, they take it all
away

So readily they gave consent when no one else
agreed
So joyfully they danced in May hoping she
wouldn't bleed
So silently, friend, winter came and took it all
away
He took it all, she took it all, they took it all
away

So eloquently he'll speak about what cannot be
put into words
So reluctantly she'll open her heart to embrace
the truth that hurts
So silently, friend, spring will come to take it all
away
He'll take it all, she'll take it all, they'll take it
all away

Far From Home

The bathwater
Lavender oil
Candles even
Worthy of a movie scene
The truth a million miles away

The fire starter
Blissful turmoil
Just like Stephen
Wondering what might have been
The truth a million miles away

The granddaughter
Another kid to spoil
Who's believing
Feeding mother's dream machine
The truth a million miles away

Defocus

He said: "You're staring at the wrong thing, shift
your focus"
How to not get sucked into what seems so real
But isn't
How to not care, how to not be so interested

What is effortless
Seems so hard
What is closer than close
Seems so far away

The suffering
Will it get you there?

Like the irritated nerve of a tooth
A constant reminder
Not okay

Seesaw

She saw the seesaw and laughed at the crackjaw
Obviously
What they put after the I am has too much
weight
And as if time was real, they wait and hurry and
wait
Quite funny this whole thing, indeed
No recollection of ever planting the seed
Did the flower bloom before it withered?
Was the possibility of error even considered?
Obviously
She saw the seesaw and laughed at the crackjaw

Knowmore Knowhere

To know more
No more cigarettes
No more alcohol
No more gambling
No more sugar
No more meat
No more identification with a false sense of self

To know where
Not here
Not there

Threads

The fabric
The threads that hold it all together
Not threatening at all
If you dare to look, look closely

Be the microscope
Let them zoom in
On the truth

Circles

A circus of sorts
Not quite as expected

All pain, no glory
Colourful presentations, yes
But shallow, oh so shallow
And no end in sight
Everyone in the circus running in circles

Maybe get a crystal ball
Predict a future that is more to your liking

Too Cozy

The fireplace
The woolen socks
Knitted with machine-like precision

Too cozy to wake up from this dream

And So It Begins

So it begins
To snow
And he thinks it's nice
It slows down the pace

Kindness begins
To show
And he thinks he's close
To winning the race

From behind the veil
Hard to see
The eternal now
And let things be

Driftwood

14

Yes, sometimes it seems that way
Spinning, freefalling

But drifting, not sinking

Blindfulness And Mindfulness

The blindful mindful dance of a thousand sons
Naked and drunk beneath a merciless merciful
sun
From every angle a different view
But do they really do what they seem to do
Up the stairs to the lookout
What about space
Not even empty
Neither this nor that
Let's see

Sixteen

Another day
Quite challenging
Tomorrow seventeen
Next year fifty

The absurdity of it all
Quite amusing
Numbers and letters
For those who care

Food

Skin and bones and cravings
Not an easy task to live without
Knowing what made us come here

The essence of everything is not found
Where you were previously looking

Wisdom from books
And cooking for freedom
From pain

For a moment

Sinking

Sinking
is more efficient
than
thinking

Let the dust settle
Let the volume drop
All the way

Uncomfortable

What does that even mean
Uncomfortable
Can't be comforted
Weird
Aren't we all

This costume feels a little tight some days
Most days, let's face it
But
Let's face it

Two Tattoos

They warned us that it would be hard
Beyond our comprehension
But that couldn't stop us
We were enthusiastic, excited, ecstatic
To go
To come here
To be this character

We agreed
To forget
Who and what we truly are

We picked
The parents
The circumstances
The hardship

He says he remembers
And I have a feeling

The two tattoos I'm getting tomorrow
Left hand, it was your choice
Right hand, it's an illusion

Holes

In the geometry of things holes are circles
And time is a line
In your face

Gaping holes everywhere
Who can help?
Yes, who
Who is taking a step in the right direction

Who's in there?
I am